Yellow Skies

Lakella Davenport

BookLeaf Publishing

India | USA | UK

Presentation by *BookLeaf Publishing*

Web: www.bookleafpub.com

E-mail: info@bookleafpub.com

ISBN: 9789360948481

First edition 2024

This book is dedicated to my late Grandmother Ms. Willie Mae Taylor. May you forever shine in the heavens above. It is because of you I know the essence of humility and a silent, yet bold strength.

The Walls

When I said I love you
I crashed into a wall.
When I said I care
My feet got stuck in the mud.
When I said things will get better
Water flowed endlessly from my eyes.
When I said God has a plan
The walls began to crack.
When I said God loves you
The walls fell down.
When I said God forgives
The grass began to grow.
When I said God gives
My cup overflowed.

On The Edge

I sit here on the edge.
The edge of despair
The edge of regret
The edge of life when it seems,
There is nothing left.
Who will lift me up?
Who will encourage me?
Who will enlighten my way?
Who will give me the words to say?
Who will fight my battles?
Who will give me a sword?
Who will fill me with an
Amazing word?
Who will help me shine
In the darkest place?
Who will bring joy to my face?
I hear a quiet still voice.
Say, I will if you only believe,
With me there is nothing
You can't achieve.

He's Been Changed

Into the water they dipped him
Out of the shame he arose.
A new creature in Christ is he.
He is no longer blind but sees.
He sees men as clear as the brown trees.
He has been converted.
All around heard it.
When he confessed his enduring faith
Shunning evil and brotherly hate
He is now presented as spiritually pure.
For Jesus is Heaven and Earth's eternal cure.

This Mother

This Mother
Sits on the front porch.
In an old wooden rocking chair
Reading through the Sunday Times
One afternoon after church
As she finishes her paper
She sips a glass of cold iced tea.
Her favorite drink in 98-degree weather
She leaves the porch
And enters the squeaky,
Clean, small, three-bedroom house
Shared by her and her
Four children and her husband Mr. Tate
She picks up a big wooden spoon
And stirs the beef stew
That's been simmering on the stove
Since early this morning
She pulls down a handful of soup bowls with
spoons
And opens the oven door with her mitts.
She grabs the pan of sweet cornbread
From the hot stove
She arranges the sweet potato pies
On the center of the long wooden dinner table.
She yells up the stairs, "Supper's ready."

Her four beautiful children
One of the best gifts the
Master in Heaven has given her
Arrive two by two and
Sit down at the table
A bowl of beef stew
Situated perfectly,
In front of their hungry bellies
Mister Tate arrives,
After the children and leads
The family in prayer and grace
One can never forget the love on This Mother's
face.

All The Pretty Flowers

All the pretty flowers
They hang delicately from the
Pot in the center of the
Ceiling
On the front porch
Such a dirty pot for
Pretty flowers
All the pretty flowers
Line up neatly in rows of
Three out in my
Grandmother's garden
One row of red roses
A second row of pink tulips
A third row of yellow daisies
A rainbow of flowers
All the pretty flowers
They sprout sparingly,
In the muddy ditch
A bunch of purple wildflowers
Laying alongside the road
In the muddy ditch
Oh! What an environment
For All the pretty flowers
Have just one wish
To brighten the lives of their possessor
With incanting merriment.

I See Dreams

I see dreams.
I see dreams,
In the middle of the
Midnight scene.
It is hard to believe
That I see dreams.
I see dreams that shadow
You and me.
I see dreams,
That long to be free.
I see dreams,
That cater to the soul.
I see dreams,
Both young and old.
I see dreams,
Left untold.
I see dreams,
Of great things to behold.
I see dreams,
That warm the cold.
I see dreams,
Not meant to be sold.
I see dreams,
That are a guiding light.
I see dreams,

In the midst of the night.
I see dreams,
Ready to take flight.
I see dreams,
Beyond human sight.

Honey To the Bee

The flowering bees have made me a pot of
honey
So delicious to my tongue
That I have to lick my
Fingers twice, no thrice
I don't want to leave any residue.
It is the most wonderful snack
When I am feeling blue
Honey on my lips
Honey on my fingertips
Honey on my plate
Honey in jars inside of old moving crates
The flowering bees have
Taken their fate.
A song of sweet joy
Not too late.

A Clustered Space, My Haven

As I look around my haven, a clustered space
To hone thoughts, ideas and creativity
I glance over at my
Handmade mahogany colored wooden desk
A gift to me from my husband
The last time I sat at it
Was for a service review
I do most of my writing
In my large queen-sized bed
Mostly because of comfort
The hard wooden desk chair is beautiful,
But leaves me in pain; if I sit too long
Resting on my desk is
my old desktop Dell computer
That doesn't work,
My three-year old's lime green, gray, and black
strapped sandals
A black and silver medicine chest also sits idle
and un-used.
Woven baskets holding body lotions, mists,
sprays,
Shower gels, rollers, hair detanglers, lip balms,
and deodorants
Blue photo album

Holding pictures of
My baby Mickey from birth to 2 years of age
Maroon photo album
Holding photos of my
Older son from birth until teenage years
Purple gratitude, prayer journal
Written Bible articles, devotional journals
Situated on top of my over stocked wooden
bookshelf
In front of the bookshelf is a red and blue toy
wagon
A green bin full of toddler toys and gadgets
Handmade three shelve bookshelf full of books
Yet, another gift from my husband
Turquoise baby walker
Baby infant bathtub given to me by my sister
Peach duffle bag holding important books
Duffle bag holding poetry, novels, and Christian
journals
Large walk-in closet
Full of male and female adult clothing
Large queen-sized bed
Beautifully stained ottoman at foot of
queen-sized bed
Inherited kitchen table
Occupying space in the extra-large master
bedroom
That I call my home seven days a week
My sacred place

White laundry basket
Inherited rocking chair
Light brown dressers overflowing with female
clothes
And toddler apparel
250 dollar Michael Kors bag
Given to me by my mother-in-law
Yellow packages of white typing paper
Box of Bic pens for writing
Boxes of Luvs pampers
Sitting on brown table
Cat litter and aluminum cans of cat food
Hidden underneath old kitchen table.

Things I Don't Know

I don't know when the world will end.
I don't know when Jesus is coming back for his
anointed.
I don't know when I will die.
I don't know Quantum Physics or advanced
Calculus.
I don't know when I will achieve all of my life's
goals.
I don't know how to fix a broken sink, or
How to tile a floor or how to do electrical work,
or
How to build a desk from scrap pieces of wood.
I don't know how to visually illustrate my
thoughts and ideas
With pictures.
I don't know how to paint the sunset or the
sunrise.
I don't know how to cure cancer.
I don't know how to change a flat tire, or
How to replace a dead battery in a car.
I don't know how to swim.
I don't know how to give up;
Because I'm constantly moving and trying,
Giving it my all no matter what.

Who Are You?

You are that blue mockingbird
Tweeting in the magnolia trees
You are that chipmunk
In the forest competing
With the brown and black squirrels for nuts.
You are that grasshopper
Eating wild berries in the summer sun.
You are that colony of ants
Storing food for the harsh winter months.
You are that cool wind
On an Autumn day,
Blowing briskly through your daughter's auburn
hair.
You are that beaver
Building the walls of a strong dam.
You are that river
That flows through the deepest valleys.
You are that flame
Shining brightly on that candle stick.
You are that northern star
Guiding travelers on their way home.
You are that field of wheat
Providing nourishment to those willing to
harvest you.
You are

Most precious and free
The glimmer of hope
That we all want to be.

Where Is God?

He is in the wind.
He is in the fire.
He is in the light.
He is in the night.
He is among the stars.
He is in a baby's first smile.
He is in the heart of every child.
He is in the clouds.
He is in the sky.
He is in you and I.
He is in the mountains.
He is in the hills.
He is in the flowers.
He is in the grass.
He is in our hearts.
He is in our minds.
He is in our spirits.
He is in the rain.
He is in the sunshine.
He is any and everywhere.

Mama's Freckles, Daddy's Face, Grandma's Faith

I hate that like you I sometimes let others walk
all over me
Without uttering a word in defense.
I am saddened because like you I tend to
Hold on to past hurts, when that person hurts me
again in the present.
It just adds to the grief I already feel for what
they've took me through
In the past.
I am happy that like both of you I have a love
for the written and spoken word.
Literature and English were subjects that both of
you excelled in
When you were in school.
Most of all I am thankful that like you, I love to
read and study the Bible, God's
Divine and ever present, holy word.
We both enjoy sharing our faith with others.
Grandmother, Mama Taylor, thanks for passing
on your
Sincere desire to give what you had to the
Church;
Even if it was only a few dollars.
Just like you I love the things of the Lord

And I pray that one day I may have the
means to give to the poor and needy
In my community or even across the world.
Sponsoring a child from an impoverished
background has been a dream of mine
Since my teenage years.
If the Lord wills, one day that dream may come
true.
Every time I look in the mirror, I see you mama.
We share the same facial freckles and round
head.
Like my dad, I have his skin tone.
My mother's skin is a number of shades lighter
than mine.
I am the only child of theirs that shares dad's
skin complexion.
My other siblings have my mama's skin
complexion.
Why did I have to be different?
Why am I darker than them?
These questions I would ask the Lord when I
was younger and naïve.
Today, it doesn't matter because I have inherited
mostly the good traits
From the ones who have given me life.

Shattered

His speech is dung.
His eyes are glass,
So fragile and easily cracked.
His heart is snow.
Falling heavily in a tight space
Who is kind enough to replace the glass?
Maybe with plastic or wood
No, not with wood,
For if it gets too hot, it will burn.

My Grandmother's Gift

A few weeks before she passed away
And went home to be with the Lord
My grandmother gave me a gift.
But my struggles in life caused me to
Throw it away after some time had passed.
It was the last gift she had given me
On one of the last times I went to visit her at
home
When she was sick, relying on oxygen to get her
through
The day and night.
A small bottle of red fingernail polish was the
gift.
Red was her favorite color.
She loved when we painted her nails.
She was such a kind, patient, and gentle soul.
I would tell her: "Grandma
I am sorry for throwing away your gift.
I wish I had it today to keep as a memorial of
you.
But I have my memories and the time we spent
together
Worshipping the Lord at your home church.
I love and miss you dearly every day.

My life seemed to literally fall apart after you
passed away.
I lost my career.
I lost my 2nd pregnancy to miscarriage at 7
weeks.
I lost my car, which I had for 4 years.
I nearly lost my mind after losing so much.
Most of all I love you.
But God remained faithful to his promises to me.
Today, I am whole and completely free.
I love you and will forever thank God for
blessing me,
With such an example of humility and peace."

My Superhero

My first born son
You are dear to my heart.
Because of the anesthesia
I bore you with very little pain
A few painless pushes
And you were out into
The strange big world
I held you on my breast
And my shoulder.
Lying in the solitary hospital room,
Thoughts raced across my mind.
"I am a mom now."
"I can't believe, I am a mom."
"What am I going to do with this little life?"
"How am I going to raise him?"
At the time I was unmarried.
I regret bearing you outside of the covenant of
marriage.
However, I don't regret giving birth to you and
Having you fill my life with so much love and
joy.
When I look at your
Batman mask with its broken headband,
I think of my first moment alone with you after
you were born.

At the age of three you developed a love for
superheroes.
I remember the countless hours you would
watch Ben 10,
At the age of four and five.
Your dad bought you that batman costume with
the mask
For you to wear when you were in HeadStart.
I remember you wearing it to school for
Halloween.
We don't celebrate Halloween anymore.
You looked just like the hero you are inside.
You had your chest out,
Bulging with confidence and joy.
I will forever keep you dear, my first-born boy.

Abundantly

He pulled me out of a pit of despair and
depression.
His gracious hand
Lifted me up when I was down.
His love was there for me when no one else was
around
My one true friend
My eternal companion
My blessed Heavenly Father
My nurturing light.
He has given me wondrous sight.
I look not to my tribulations; but to the hills
which cometh my help.
I keep my eyes fixed on him.
Jesus, Jesus
Is your name.
With you I will never be the same
My heart you have tamed.
I know that I am abundantly changed.

A King Is Born!

25

A King is born!
A King is born!
Come and see!
His glorious star
Set in the East
The wise men have brought him gifts.
A savior of all mankind
Let this news bring you peace of mind.
Holy, humble, and meek
Is the King we truly seek
Jesus is his marvelous name.
He was put here to do wondrous things.
Oh! What salvation and joy he brings!

Immeasurable

You're unchangeable.
You're faithful,
In all that you do.
You're true to all,
Both small and great.
You are a God of worthy faith.
Who could ask for a better Father
A better healer
A better friend
A better provider
Than you
A God of war
A God of peace
A God of mercy
A God of justice
A God of Faith
A God of love
A God of Dreams
A God over all the earth.
Immeasurable is your divine worth.

In The Nightshade

In the night shade
I watch the picket fence fade.
I see the diming lights one or two per street
As the moon's shadow bounces off my feet
As I sit, quietly still, in my father's backseat.
Mama looks back with glowing eyes
As my baby brother fusses and cries
What is a matter with him this time?
Mama passes me a warm bottle of cow's milk.
She is beautifully dressed in pink silk.
I am dressed in your average pre-teen years.
For my courtesy I deserve
A handclap of cheers
I rarely succumb to my daily fears.
I am happy sitting in the night shade.
Watching eagerly as my childhood slowly fades.

Aim To Be God's Reflection

Aim to be God's reflection.
A picture of his goodness
And all things great
There is nothing under the sun he didn't create.
Make sure you leave a space in your heart
For him to dwell and be apart
Imitate his kindness and his joy
Imitate his peace and his long-suffering
Imitate his forgiveness and his mercy
Imitate his will power and his self-control
Let his presence help you grow
Continue to reap and sow
Aim to be God's reflection!
A mirror image of all that's virtuous and noble
within you.

My People

My people stand strong.
My people don't worry long.
My people embrace each wave.
My people are crying to be saved.
My people understand the notion of right.
My people stand, ready to fight.
My people fight with their words.
My people fight until they are heard.
My people dance underneath the moon.
My people shake the air in the room.
My people will break free soon.
My people are banners of light.
My people can see beyond the darkest nights.
My people sing in the cool of the day.
My people kneel down and pray.
My people have found their way.